THE STORY OF LOWESTOFT LIFEBOATS - PART 1. 1801-1876

THE STORY OF LOWESTOFT LIFEBOATS

PART 1 1801-1876

by
Jack Mitchley

LOWESTOFT LIBRARIES

This edition published 1974 by
Lowestoft Libraries
in Association with
Port of Lowestoft Research Society

© J. W. Mitchley 1973
Previous edition 1973

ISBN   0   904328   00   7

Printed by Wavney District Council, Town Hall, Lowestoft, Suffolk

CONTENTS

Greathead's Boat	1801-1807	page 2
Frances Ann	1807-1850	8
Victoria	1850-1869	19
Laetitia	1869-1876	25
Index		29

Cover picture from a lithograph by William Joy
depicting launch of the Frances Ann date 1821

INTRODUCTION

Very little has appeared in print about Lowestoft's first lifeboat. Fortunately Robert Sparrow of Worlingham Hall, one of the founders of the Lifeboat Society which owned the boat, wrote a number of letters about it to the Ipswich Journal. With the help of these letters, and the report of the Parliamentary Committee held in 1802 to consider if Greathead, who built the boat, should receive a Parliamentary Grant, I have been able to put together what I believe is an accurate and fairly complete account of this unfortunate boat.

Her successor, the **Frances Ann**, is much better known. Not only was she the first lifeboat in the world built to use sails as well as oars, she was also the forerunner of the famous Norfolk & Suffolk type, a non self-righting design used almost exclusively on the East Anglian coast for over 130 years. The Northumberland Report on lifeboats, published in 1851 credits her with having saved 300 lives in her 43 years service. Unfortunately, the most thorough search of the Norwich and Ipswich weekly papers fails to reveal details of more than about a quarter of her launches.

This story first appeared as supplements to the Research Society's Newsletters, but has been corrected and amended as further information has been received.

Finally, I would like to thank R. W. Malster of Ipswich and Grahame Farr of Bristol for help over details of some of the launches, and E. D. Porter of Lowestoft for information about the local beachmen.

J. W. Mitchley

50, Kirkley Cliff,
LOWESTOFT

March 1973

GREATHEAD'S BOAT 1801-07

ALTHOUGH a gale was raging, and a number of vessels in the roads were flying signals of distress in their rigging, the lifeboat remained on the beach. The pilots and beachmen were out in their own boats giving all the assistance possible, but none of them could be persuaded to use the strange new boat.

This lifeboat had been built by Henry Greathead at Shields. It was a wooden pulling boat, double ended, rowing ten oars, thirty feet long, with a beam of ten feet six inches and was steered by an oar at either end. Its arrival at Lowestoft on February 27th, 1801, was the culmination of much hard work by Robert Sparrow of Worlingham Hall, near Beccles, by the Revd. Francis Bowness of Lowestoft*, and a few more local gentlemen. Having heard much of the benefits of the lifeboats which were already in use in the North of England, they formed a Lifeboat Society which was instituted on the sixth of September, 1800, and set in being a subscription fund to finance a similar boat, to be stationed at Lowestoft. These funds came from many sources. Trinity House contributed £52-10-0d. the Duke of Rutland, Marquis Cornwallis, Lord Brome, Sir Thomas and Lady Beauchamp, squires, parsons and the man in the street all made contributions. One of the subscription lists also shows that several parishes made donations as follows:—

Henstead	£1- 7-0d.	Wrentham	£ 6- 6-0d.
Kessingland	£5- 5-0d	Worlingham	£ 5-13 6d
Barton	£2- 7 0d	Ereswell	£ 1-16-6d
Lakenheath	£2- 5 0d	Heringswell	£ 1-11-6d
Wangford	£1- 1-0d	Brandon	£ 1-10-6d
Tuddenham	£ 17-6d	Cavenham	£ 10-0d
Freckenham	£2-16-0d	Kennet	£ 1- 1-0d
Newmarket	£3- 3-0d	Exning	£ 1- 1-0d
Chippenham	£2-12-0d	Mildenhall	£13-13-0d

In the 'Ipswich Journal' of March the seventh, the editor had the "pleasure to inform the benevolent subscribers to the Lifeboat that one of these vessels arrived at Lowestoft yesterday se'nnight". On the following Monday, twelve men took her out to sea "to practise a number of manoeuvres", and as a result, "in the opinion of the best judges, she is well calculated to answer the purpose intended".

Although the boat was called the **Lowestoft Lifeboat** its usefulness was to be extended to the North and South of the town, "as far as may be consistent with safety". Her cost has been given as £105 but this is probably a misprint for £165, which was the cost of the ten-oared boat (his biggest model), according to Greathead in evidence before a Parliamentary Committee in 1802.

Father Bowness was the Rector of Gunton.

Page, in his "County History of Suffolk", quoting from Martin's "History of Lloyds", states that Lloyds put a lifeboat here in 1802. E. R. Cooper, the noted Southwold historian, and Honorary Secretary of the lifeboat there for many years, unable to find trace of the 1801 boat, considers it was probably confused with the one stated to have been sent here by Lloyds as an experiment. (Suffolk Coast Garland). Lloyds, however, did not send a lifeboat here, or anywhere else.

On July 23rd, 1802, a General Meeting of Subscribers to Lloyd's placed a sum of £2,000 at the disposal of the Committee for the purpose of encouraging the building of lifeboats for different parts of the United Kingdom, but the parties applying for a grant for this purpose were to man and maintain the boats at their own expense. In August, Lloyds received a letter from the Revd. Richard Frank of Alderton, near Woodbridge, requesting the assistance of the Committee "towards defraying the expense of the two lifeboats already established on the Suffolk coast, at Lowestoft and Hollesey Bay", and a sum of thirty pounds was voted for the Lowestoft boat and fifty pounds for the Hollesey Bay boat.

The method of launching the boat was described by Captain Gilfred Lawson Reed to a committee of the House of Commons in 1802. This committee had been convened to consider a petition by Greathead for a Parliamentary grant and Captain Reed, who was an Elder Brother of Trinity House and had the management of the lifeboat at Lowestoft in 1801, was one of a number of persons called upon to give evidence. In his evidence he said that after fitting her for service as far as he thought proper, he was requested by a number of subscribers to launch the boat, which he did on a very rough day, when the sea fell very heavy on the beach, and in the presence of about two hundred spectators. "Twenty-four men jumped into her and when she first mounted the waves, the spectators with one voice expressed their astonishment". He had given the men orders to cross the shoal that lay about one and a half miles from the shore and upon which the sea broke heavily, but by some mistake one of the plugs was left out of the bottom of the boat and she filled with water before reaching the shoal. The men returned safely, "though when she gained the shore, she was full of water to the gunwale amidships, yet, by her sheare, one third of her at each end was out of the water".

At first they had to drag the boat by four or five horses, with a rope through the boats stem. This split the stem, which had to be reinforced with iron plates. Also, it took about an hour to launch. Soon afterwards a launching carriage was constructed to Greathead's design. This consisted of four wheels or rollers, upon which the boat was dragged to the edge of the water.

Captain Reed then went on to give a description of the method of launching and recovering the boat. "The distance from the boathouse to the shore is one hundred yards and the boat's crew can run her down in ten minutes. When the sea does not tumble in upon the beach very much the boat may be easily launched, by laying the ways as far as possible in the water and the carriage hauled from under her; when there is a great sea upon the beach, the boat must be launched from the carriage before she comes to the surf, on planks laid across, as other boats are launched, the people standing on the ends to prevent the sea moving them, then, with the assistance of the anchor and cable (which had been laid out to sea for that purpose), the boats crew would draw her over the highest sea".

When asked what he thought made the boat superior to any other ever invented, he replied:— "the curvature of the keel and the flaunching sides which rendered it almost impossible to be upset. When the boat was afloat and full of water, the men all went to one side of the boat in order to try and upset her, which they could not effect. The cork must certainly be considered to be an essential part of the boat".

During the enquiry Captain Reed was asked whether he knew Mr. Johnson, a shipwright of Lowestoft, and whether he had not said that he would build a lifeboat for much less money than was charged by Mr. Greathead. He replied that he had not heard Mr. Johnson make such a remark, nor did he know that the man was a shipbuilder. When asked if he was aware that a patent had been granted to Mr. Lukin, coach-maker, for making a boat (built by Hodges of Lambeth) buoyant by cork, for the purpose of saving mariners in distress, Captain Reed said he had no knowledge of it.

In spite of favourable reports on the lifeboat from other places, the local men would not use her. In October 1804 a letter addressed to "the pilots, sailors and seafaring men of the town of Lowestoft" appeared in the Ipswich Journal, complaining about this lack of use. Although unsigned the letter would appear to have been written by Robert Sparrow, Esq., one of the original promoters, who remarks that:— "Two circumstances of contrary nature attend the situation at Lowestoft; one, that it is very fortunate in the frequency of seafaring men, used to all bodily exertions and who already had shown their intrepidity and generosity in assisting distress, the other, that by the lack of a creek, there was difficulty in getting out to the sea when the winds were much contrary; this difficulty has been in part obviated, the Government having supplied a cable and hawser (anchor?) at the instance of the late Lord Henneker".

He goes on to ask " whence comes it then that the lifeboat operating with so much success in all other places, is at Lowestoft an object of dislike, that so far from resorting to her when opportunities offer, few occassions are lost to lower her services in the opinion of the public?". After mentioning that the Bawdsey boat during the previous winter had saved six or eight lives from one launch, he goes on "To endeavour to rouse you from the languid state in which you are, or from the disgraceful prejudice you have adopted, I offer you, from the remainder of the subscription left in my hands, a reward of ten guineas for every exertion, fairly and fully made, with the lifeboat, and if the exertion be attended with the success of saving human life, the reward shall be extended to fifteen guineas — it rests with you to bring this fortunate system forward; should my present attempt fail, I shall first state the failure to the public, and then look for a situation where a more worthy race of men will gladly accept the advantages you have blindly refused".

His attempt did fail, but Robert Sparrow did not mention the fact at the time and only a small paragraph in the Ipswich Journal of 25th January, 1806, mentions that the lifeboat had been removed from Lowestoft to Gorleston, "for the sake of the haven". The move was a failure, as Sparrow later admits in a letter in the Ipswich Journal of 24th October, 1807. Apologising to the subscribers to the lifeboat fund for the delay in telling them what had been going on, and for the absence of a statement of accounts, he says that this is partly due to the death of his colleague, the Revd. Mr. Bowness, "from whose humanity the attempt had originated". Refering to the lifeboat, he pointed out that although she was fitted out in the same manner as the other lifeboats used elsewhere, nothing could reconcile her to the pilots and beachmen of Lowestoft, who were to use her, and the difficulty of getting her out to sea with an adverse wind appeared to increase the dislike.

"I removed her to Gorleston, upon the haven, where she might be launched with great ease in a short time, but here also the same dislike attended her, and when, in a late terrible storm the scene of distress was so great as to induce some humane gentlemen to offer twenty guineas as a reward for the use of the lifeboat, the refusal at once convinced me that nothing was ever to be expected from her from this part of the coast".

In spite of this setback, Robert Sparrow does not give up hope. "Mr. Lukin, a gentlemen who has made the system of lifeboats his particular study, has written a treatise upon the subject, and received a patent for a lifeboat as long ago as the year 1785, was fortunately at that time resident in Lowestoft, and the many conversations he had with the sailors there, produced the following letter addressed to me:—

Lowestoft, September 21st, 1807

"Sir,

We whose names are hereunto subscribed, pilots of Lowestoft, being informed you are desirous that the lifeboat brought hither from Shields should be altered and improved so as to be more suitable for this coast, or that a new one should be built in such a form as we, by our experience, judge most likely to answer the intended purpose, beg leave to assure you, Sir, that our disapprobation of the Shields boat arises from no other cause than her unfitness for these shores, on account of her form which may be very servicable on a flat coast, but totally unserviceable on this steep shore, where it cannot possibly be launched through a heavy surf without being filled and when full of water becomes so heavy as to be quite unmanageable.

How far any alteration may remove these objections, we are not able positively to determine, but are of the opinion they can only be partially removed, and that a new one may be constructed to answer the purpose much better, both as to safety and management; but whatever boat shall be stationed on this coast as a lifeboat by the subscribers, we hereby declare, that we shall, and we believe all our fraternity will be ready at all times to use it for the purpose intended, in preference to our own, provided we are convinced, by proper experiments, that such a boat is manageable here, and that she will not sink if filled with water, in addition to her proper burthen — this being a degree of safety which we confess our yawls do not possess.

We are etc...............
(39 names)".
(unfortunately the names were not printed).

Robert Sparrow continues:- "Mr. Lukin also offered to remain purposely at Lowestoft and superintend either the alteration of the present boat, or the construction of a new one upon his own principle; those he had discussed with the sailors, and I found they approved them; the objections they made to the old lifeboat went to every part of her; the alterations necessary to bring her into favour were calculated at about one hundred pounds, and even then the event appeared very doubtful. On the other hand the pilots pointed out their favourite boat, in which they had made many daring exertions, and declared, if such a one was provided for them and made secure in buoyancy, and not liable to be overset, they would gladly engage to use her - the expense was calculated at about two hundred pounds. A larger sum than this remained in my hands from the former subscriptions, a statement of which shall be laid before the public. It was not possible for me to call the subscribers together, or by any means to collect their sentiments; time pressed very much."

"Mr. Lukin's time was also valuable to him, and I was to make an immediate determination. In this difficulty, how to act; the only step I could take was to apply to Trinity House, who had been liberal in their assistance of money and advice, and the answer of Captain Reed, an Elder Brother of that body, to whom I had addressed my letter, determined me, at my own risque, to hazard the approbation of a liberal public, in ordering a new boat to be built at Lowestoft, similar to that requested by the pilots, and according to the principles and under the constant inspection of Mr. Lukin. Should this attempt be attended with the desired success, it will be for the public to determine how far it will be proper to provide a moderate fund for rewards and repairs."

Worlingham Hall, October 15th, 1807   Robert Sparrow

The Ipswich Journal of the following 14th November carried an advertisement for the sale of the old lifeboat-"her form not suiting the steepness of the shore." The boat was lying in the yard of Mr. Barcham, boatbuilder, and was to be sold with "twelve oars with grummets, and two staves, eight billedge planks for a road, and a carriage with four wheels to move the boat upon."

Five days later, on the 19th November, an important event took place close to where the rejected lifeboat lay. The first Lowestoft-built lifeboat was launched.

About eighteen months prior to this , a new Society had been formed. Some of the promoters were members of the Lifeboat Society, and the new Society was soon closely connected with the Lowestoft Lifeboat, so this is probably the best point at which to introduce them into the story. The Ipswich Journal of 22nd February, 1806, contained the following letter:-

Suffolk Humane Society

The Right Honourable, Lord Rous, President. Resolved:

That in consequence of the numerous accidents to which the Eastern Coast is particularly exposed, it is highly expedient to institute a Society on the principles of the Royal Humane Society of London, and that the Gentlemen whose names are subscribed to these resolutions to constitute such a Society, with the addition of as many others as shall be willing to become members of the same.

That this Society shall consist of a President, Vice-presidents, Treasurers and Secretaries, and that the Rt. Hon. Lord Rous* be President, the Rt. Hon. Lord Huntingfield, Sir John Blois, Bart., Sir Thomas Gooch, Bart., and Robert Sparrow, Esq., be Vice-presidents; the Revd. B. Bence and the Revd. R. Lockwood Treasurers, and the Revd. W. Spurdens and the Revd. M. Maurice, Secretaries.

That this Society be distinguished by the name of the Suffolk Humane Society.

That the exertions and rewards of this Society shall in the first instance embrace a district including the Hundreds of Mutford and Lothingland, Blything and Wangford; and the other Hundreds be invited to unite themselves with this Society.

That this Society will reward any persons who admit a body under suspended animation into his house; and also all those who shall be instrumental in rescuing it from the water, or promoting its recovery. That the object of the Society shall also extend to the application of whatever means may most effectually awaken the exertions of humanity, particularly among the peasantry on the coast, in cases of shipwreck.

* *Lord Rous later became the first Earl of Stradbroke*

That subscriptions for these purposes be solicited; and that every annual subscriber of ten shillings and sixpence shall be a Governor; and shall be entitled to vote in all the concerns of this Society.

That any five or more Governors in the neighbourhood of the place where any accident shall occur within the views of the Society, shall consitute a Committee of Reward; and shall be empowered to distribute the remunerations of the Society, having previously obtained the concurrance of the President, one of the Vice-presidents, one of the Treasurers, and one of the Secretaries.

That the medical gentlemen, members of this Society be requested to form themselves into a committee for the purpose of framing such instructions as they shall judge beneficial for promoting the ends of the Society.

That bankers in Yarmouth and in the County of Suffolk be requested to receive subscriptions in aid of the purposes of this Society.

That a Public Meeting be held on Monday the third of March next, at the King's Head, Beccles, at 12 o'clock in the forenoon, for the purposes of framing laws and regulations, and giving permanent form to the Society; where the presence of every person is requested, who may wish to countenance so laudable and necessary an institution.

W. SPURDENS, Clerk. Secretary.

FRANCES ANN 1807-50

Lowestoft 19th November. "THIS DAY WAS LAUNCHED THE FRANCES ANN, lifeboat, built at this place under the direction of Mr. Lukin of Long Acre, London. The weather was very unfavourable incessant and heavy rain falling all the day; from this cause the number of persons assembled was not so great as it would have been, though some gentlemen animated by the noble wish of promoting means of saving the lives of fellow creatures, came from a considerable distance to witness the success of the undertaking."

So began the long and detailed account of the event printed in the Norwich and Ipswich papers of the 28th November, 1807.

No doubt one of the gentlemen who braved the elements was Lord Rous, President of the Suffolk Humane Society, after whose seventeen year old daughter the boat was named. It would be nice to think that the young lady herself performed the naming ceremony, but of this there is no record.

The **Frances Ann** was a sailing lifeboat, the first of her kind in this country, probably in the world, and she might never have been built if Lukin had not decided to come to Lowestoft for a holiday Both Mr. Lukin and his son prolonged their stay in the town for some weeks, just to superintend her construction. She was built on the North Beach by Batchelor Barcham, already well known as a boat builder. Forty foot long, with a beam of ten foot four inches and a depth of only three foot one inch, she was rowed by fourteen oars and weighed five tons. In the report of her launch she was described as having "an iron keel which serves her for ballast, with a contrivance of casks placed at her bottom to be filled with water when necessary to increase her ballast; other air casks for the purpose of buoyancy and to prevent her sinking though filled with water, are placed round her inside. She also has projecting gunwales cased with cork, with concealed air boxes. Her air casks were copper bound, and attached by rope to eye bolts."

Designed on the lines of the beachman's favourite beach yawl, she probably had three masts, although an engraving of 1820 shows her with only two. It is possible that like some of the yawls she left her mainmast ashore in the winter months. In colour she was a bright varnish, with the characteristic glowing cork belt. Some sources give her cost as £105, but the Northumberland report gives it as £200, which is also the figure estimated by Robert Sparrow in his letter of 15th October, 1807. (See page 6).

A lady who wrote a "Guide to Lowestoft" published in 1812, was much impressed by the lifeboat, and wrote of her "This boat is so admirably constructed as not only to be able to brave every inclemency of weather, but to bid defiance to the most turbulent waves; for were it even to upset it is so judiciously formed that it would right itself again immediately, thus the brave and generous sailors who volunteer to rescue their fellow creatures from a watery grave, being securely lashed to the sides of this vessel may pursue their course fearless of danger, as it is impossible she can ever sink. A swinging cot with every convenience and accommodation appertains to this lifeboat, in order to conduct the exhausted sufferers who may stand in need of assistance, with safety to the shore. In a boathouse situate on the beach towards the lower end of the town (which was built expressly to contain the lifeboat, her masts, rigging, etc.) is likewise placed Captain Manby's apparatus."

The good lady must have been slightly misinformed by an over enthusiastic supporter of the lifeboat, for the **Frances Ann** was not a self-righter, nor was she unsinkable. She was however, as safe as any boat could be made, and it was hoped that the men who used her would be able to do so "with a confidence of security to which they had been unaccustomed."

She was launched at mid-day with sixteen persons on board. A heavy rain was falling and the south-easterly wind was increasing in strength. She sailed round for a while until the crew got the feel of her then she made for the north end of the Corton Sands, on which the surf was running very high, and ran the whole length upon the sands without shipping any water. Coming off the sands the plugs were removed and the water allowed to rise as far as the air casks would allow. The **Frances Ann** then sailed up to Pakefield, her progress apparently unaffected by the water in her bottom. To test her stability, all sixteen men on board got over to the leeward side and some of them stood on her gunwale, yet from all their weight, the press of sail, and the plugs still open, her side was not depressed, nor did the water increase inside the boat. (This test was repeated every year at the General Meeting of the Suffolk Humane Society.) Coming back near the shore, she was completely filled with water by means of buckets, and four more men got into her from another boat, but she still floated easily. It was estimated that she would be able to hold fifty persons with safety, even when filled with water.

The **Frances Ann** was the forerunner of a class of lifeboat which became known as the Norfolk and Suffolk type, a non self-righting design preferred by the beachmen on this part of the coast and used almost exclusively on the Norfolk, Suffolk and Essex coasts for well over one hundred and thirty years. Lowestoft's last boat of the class was the **Agnes Cross** built in 1921 as the **John and Mary Meiklam of Gladswood**. She was replaced by a "Watson" boat, the **Michael Stephens** in 1939. The last Norfolk & Suffolk type to be built was the **Mary Scott**, built in 1925 for Southwold. She was sold out of the service in 1953 and became a private yacht.

The **Frances Ann** made her first service launch on the 24th February, 1808, being launched to a boat aground on the sands off Lowestoft (probably Corton Sands). The wind and tide being against the Lowestoft boats - yawls has also launched - Gorleston yawls got to the vessel first. They did not attempt to board her until the Lowestoft lifeboat was very near. Then, afraid that they might loose their prize, they made the attempt. No further launch is recorded until the end of 1809, when, on 14th December, she went out in a "tremendous" gale. The beach was strewn with wreck and many vessels were ashore between Lowestoft and Yarmouth. The **Catherine** - Mackenzie, master - of and from Sunderland, with coals for Chatham, upset on the Holm Sands off the town. As soon as it was known that there was a survivor on the wreck, the lifeboat was launched, and with great difficulty managed to rescue him. He was the ship's carpenter, and in the rescue, unfortunately had several ribs broken. The Norwich Mercury about a month later reported that the crew who had carried out this rescue, had received the thanks of the committee of the Suffolk Humane Society, and rejoiced to add that the carpenter was recovered from the injury occasioned by the wreck, and now enabled to return to his friends.

Eleven months later, on the 10th November, 1810, what was described as a "most tremendous gale" visited the coast. Four vessels were driven ashore at Corton, the **Echo** of and from North Shields; the **Hoggett** from London; the **Maria** of and from Newcastle; and the **Sylph** of and from Sunderland. All the crews were saved, many by Manby's apparatus. Another vessel was driven on the sands opposite the town, and the crew took to the rigging. The lifeboat was hauled down to the water, but the beachmen were unwilling to launch, even when twenty-five guineas were offered by some gentlemen who were present. They claimed that the danger was very great, and anyway they had not been paid for former services. The report of the incident published later in the Ipswich paper remarks - "it is to be observed however that the best sailors were engaged at Corton".

Although the lifeboat had proved its capabilities, the beachmen still prefered their yawls. If no arrangements had been made with the various groups of beachmen about manning the lifeboat, it would be their natural reaction when trouble was reported, to run to their own yawls. As these were kept near their sheds, which were close to their lookouts, they could be launched in a very short time. As an observer once wrote of them, "they know a ship is on the sands before the ship's crew know it, and they launch their boats and are half way to the rescue before the crew know in what jeopardy they are."

The lifeboat however, was housed at the south end of the town near her builder's yard. By the time the beachmen had assembled, the crew picked, the gear put into the boat, and the boat launched, yawls could be well on their way to the casualty. Only when the seas were too rough to risk their yawls could their rivalry be overcome sufficiently to get them to work together in the lifeboat.

This was illustrated by the next recorded launch of the **Frances Ann.**

Near the lighthouse at the top end of the town was the pilot lookout, this being about the highest point on the coast. When a vessel was seen on the sands off Corton early one Friday morning in January, 1815, three pilot yawls were launched to investigate. Approaching the wreck, which proved to be the sloop **Jeanie** of Hull, bound for London with a cargo of potatoes, they saw three men still on it. At the same time they saw that the surf and broken water surrounding the wreck made it impossible for them to get near it in their yawls, so a signal was made to the shore and the lifeboat was launched. The crew consisted of four pilots, Henry May, David Burwood, James Cullingham jnr, and Henry Beverley Disney and fourteen beachmen - Cornelius Ferrett, William Ayres, Samuel Spurden, James Spurden, Robert Watson, James Websdale jnr., Bartholmew Allerton, James Farrer jnr, Peter Smith, George Burwood, Matthew Colman, Edward Ellis jnr., and James Stebbens.

A graphic description of the rescue was later written by the Revd. Bartholmew Ritson, Curate of the Parish Church*, and secretary of the Suffolk Humane Society.

"The alacrity with which these brave fellows leaped on board the lifeboat is hardly to be described. After encountering much difficulty and danger in passing through the breakers, they came near the vessel in sight of hundreds

* *Fr. Ritson was Perpetual Curate of Hopton and for 37 years Assistant Curate of Lowestoft. He died in 1835 and is buried in the churchyard at Lowestoft Parish Church.*

of spectators who from the heights were beholding with astonishment their nautical skill and their dauntless courage; at the same time trembling between hope and fear for their safety, and lifting up a silent prayer for the successful termination of their perilous undertaking. Heaven in its mercy smiled propitious upon their endeavours, and rewarded the exertions of these brave men with success; they having the heartfelt satisfaction of bringing the three shipwrecked mariners to shore without a single accident".

Lloyds List for Tuesday, 17th January, 1815 reports- "The **Jane,** Nailer, of and from Hull to London, was lost on Corton Sand on Friday. The crew were saved by the lifeboat from Lowestoft."

The Suffolk Humane Society promptly voted the lifeboat crew the sum of five guineas, and the Secretary concluded the report of the incident by claiming that a "most favourable opportunity has been afforded the Suffolk Humane Society of proving to the public the complete safety and consequent utility of the Lowestoft lifeboat; that with it has been happily effected as far as human means can avail that which could not have been effected by any other boat from the beach; and what is more desirable, all those doubts respecting its eligibility as a sea boat have been cleared up, and all prejudices to its disadvantage which have been known to exist in the minds of our seafaring men removed".

The next four years, from 1816 until 1819, had their quota of gales, with the usual tale of ships ashore or on the various sands, and although yawls were out many times, there is no record of the lifeboat being used. There was still prejudice and suspicion about. In fact, in 1819 not only the lifeboat, but the Suffolk Humane Society itself came under attack from an anonymous writer, and unfortunately it was not until October of 1820 that the Society was able to answer the "Anonymous scribbler" as they called him.

On Sunday morning, 22nd October, 1820, there raged a heavy gale from the south-south-west, which towards noon increased to almost a hurricane. Two boats which tried to gain the Inner Roads, through the Stanford Channel, struck the Beacon Ridge and vanished in the space of a few minutes. A third vessel, the sloop **Sarah & Caroline,** of Woodbridge, struck the Newcome and filled. Her masts remained standing and the crew of five took to the rigging. As it was only half ebb, with a tremendously strong wind, the lifeboat, when she was launched, was towed a considerable way to the southward to bring her on a bearing with the vessel in distress. When the tow was let go, however, she fell to leeward, and it was not until the tide began to turn that they made headway against the wind. After the most presevering and strenuous exertions they succeeded in gaining the wreck, and took the five men from the rigging.

On their way to the **Sarah & Caroline** the lifeboat had been hailed by a brig, which was boarded on the return from the sloop. This vessel proved to be the **George** of London, John Dixon, Master, with coal and a crew of six. She was waterlogged. The crew were all taken into the lifeboat, and, at about six o'clock in the evening, the twelve survivors were safely landed on Lowestoft beach. The sloop's mast fell about half an hour after the men had left it and the brig sank soon afterwards.

The lifeboat this time was under the command of Lieutenant Samuel Thomas Carter, R.N., who had as crew pilots H. B. Disney, James Stebbens, and James Titlow and the beachmen Thomas Aldiss, Henry Smith, Thomas Butcher, William Hook, William Gurney, James Taylor, John Browne, William Francis, Robert Chaston, Edward Boyce, Thomas Humsley, Nathanial Kilwick, James Robinson and William Butcher.

This rescue was commemorated by the well known engraving which was published soon after, showing the **Frances Ann** going off to the vessel with the crew in the rigging. The date under the picture was incorrectly given as 1821 instead of 1820. The fine work of the lifeboat also gave the secretary of the Suffolk Humane Society a chance to answer those who still critised the lifeboat and anything to do with it.

"About a year ago, those who had the care and conduct of the lifeboat were most unjustly and petulantly assailed by an anonymous writer. The present instance however, it is hoped will convince the public that all reports to the disadvantage either of the boat or its conductors (particularly such as raised by anonymous scribblers), are totally void of foundation; of this occasion moreover has been most forcibily demonstrated the utility of the lifeboats in general, when properly constructed, and of that of Lowestoft in particular, that as far as human means are available, she is fully adequate to the humane purpose for which she is intended, and that in her, as in the instance now related may be done what in any other boat or yawl, it would be the extreme rashness to attempt".

In spite of this further proof of her usefulness, the **Frances Ann** remained on the beach. If a casualty was sighted, it was still the gigs and yawls which went out.

On 7th December 1821 the brig **Westmoreland** of Stockton, Thomas Ryder, master, was bound for London through the Stanford Channel. It was nearly low water. In coming to leeward she struck the Stanford Sand and unhung her rudder. Becoming unmangeable, she went onto the Newcome Sand and promptly hoisted a distress signal in the main rigging. Two gigs put off to her assistance, followed by two yawls, and later by the lifeboat. The gigs found when they got to the vessel that the surf was too much for them, so laid off for the yawls to come up. The first one to do so hestiated and gave her rival, the **Seaman's Assistance**, the chance she needed to get alongside first, and two of her crew boarded the brig.

A little later the lifeboat came up, and although the crew of the yawl told them that everything was under control and their assistance was not needed, made fast alongside the **Westmoreland,** only to have her rope cut by someone on board the brig. About five minutes later, under the combined efforts of the crews of the brig and the yawl, the brig was afloat. It was then found that she was making water fast, so she was beached on the 'flats' opposite the Common Style (now Claremont Road). The beachmen, knowing that nothing could now save the vessel, tried to persuade the crew to leave the boat and come ashore. A few of the crew and a woman passenger, described as the Captain's wife, left the ship, but the Captain and five other refused. Later, finding that there were still men on the wreck, the lifeboat again went out, but could not get near enough owing to the lack of water. Some of the crew of the **Seaman's Assistance**, seeing the trouble, took out one of their skiffs, hired some horses and took the skiff through the town. They then floated her, and taking on board, at his own request a Lieutenant Harmer, managed to get out to the wreck. The Lieutenant just managed to spring on board when the skiff was nearly swamped and forced away from the wreck. A second boat, which had followed managed to take the officer and two men off and land them safely. The Captain, it seems, had been killed by a blow from the boom, or from some other cause, whilst three other men, finding their mistake out too late had tried to get ashore in the ship's boat and were lost. The body of the Captain was later brought ashore and buried in the Churchyard at Kirkley Parish Church.

The law took a serious view of the lifeboat having been cut adrift, as it resulted in the death of the Captain. The yawl's crew of fifteen were arrested and taken to London for trial. Several were sentenced to a period in Newgate Jail, including John Stebbins jnr., Benjamin Cook and Nathanial Kilwick. If this report is correct, the sentence must have been very short because Stebbins was out again in the yawl in March, 1822.

All that is known of the next launch is that the Suffolk Association for the Preservation of Lives of Shipwrecked Seamen awarded £28-7-0d. to the crew of the Lowestoft lifeboat for the rescue of the crew of the **Ann** on 18th January, 1825.

On the same day, the lifeboat was also out to the Ramsgate sloop **Dorset,** which had grounded on the Holm Sands. Whilst laying alongside the wreck in an unballasted condition, the **Frances Ann** was suddenly overwhelmed by a big sea, and before the crew could pull out the plugs to give her the designed stability when flooded and free her of the superflouous water, she was completely awash to the gunwales. Fortunately she survived this and her crew were unscathed, but some of the sloop's crew were unfortunately lost.

On the twentieth of October in the same year (1825) the **Rochester** of North Shields was seen in a very dangerous position on the Corton Sand, to the north-east of the town. At about 7.45 a.m. the lifeboat was launched through very heavy seas. Although it was ebb tide, the wind was strong from the nor-nor-east and with such tremendous squalls that the boat could make little headway. After tacking on and off for about an hour, she was run ashore.

Immediately re-manned, she was launched again and towed along the shore to windward as far as Corton Rails. Casting off, the boat reached toward Corton Sand, weathering the wreck by nearly a quarter of a mile, but she was now too late. The ship was laying with her masts in the water, and the survivors had been washed from their hold.

The Suffolk Humane Society voted ten shillings and sixpence to each of the eighteen men in the lifeboat and the larger sum of one pound to Samuel Allerton who had reported the wreck.

In May, 1828, the brig **Fawn** of Sunderland, Bamborough master, was on her way from her home port to London with coals, when on the seventeenth she drove on to the Corton Sand in a strong east-nor-east wind. Two Yarmouth yawls were launched to her assistance, but when they reached her they found the crew had left in their own boat and, because of the heavy seas, they decided not to board her. People on the shore, seeing the yawls returning, thought that the crew had been left on board, so the Yarmouth lifeboat was launched. The Lowestoft lifeboat had also been launched to the **Fawn's** assistance and they found the crew in their own boat, which had passed safely over the sand and through the broken water.

Several vessels were in trouble in Lowestoft Roads in November of the following year. On the twenty-third, a Monday, a tremendous gale began to blow, which continued until late on Wednesday. On the Monday, the collier brig **Thomas and Mary** of Newcastle, Wilson master, with coals, went on the south end of the Newcome Sand. The lifeboat, after crossing the Newcome, ran to windward of the vessel, anchored, veered down to her, and although the heavy seas were breaking over both vessels, managed to take off the master, eight men and a boy.

The next morning with the wind hard east by north, two brigs riding off Pakefield were seen flying distress signals. While the lifeboat was being prepared for launching, one brig was seen to slip her anchor and run for the beach. The lifeboat, again under Lieutenants, Harmer and Carter and with twenty in the crew, launched to the second brig, which was the **Ann** of London, David Walker master. Using the same tactics as on the previous day, the master and nine men were safely taken off the vessel, which a few hours later came ashore and was completely wrecked on Kirkley beach. The two officers received the thanks of the Suffolk Humane Society, whilst the crew received five pounds.

A number of other vessels came ashore on the beaches, where the crews were saved by the beachmen.

A year later, on November 26th, 1830, the brig **Clifton**, bound from Hamburg to London, W. Walker master, got herself on the Corton Sand, almost opposite the floating light. This vessel was carrying a mixed cargo of furs, wool etc. Lieutenant Carter, who was in charge of the **Frances Ann,** as soon as he was informed of the incident, launched to her assistance and rescued the crew of nine as well as one passenger. Thirteen bales of wool, and two pianos were saved from the wreck and on the fifth of January 1831, Thomas Balls auctioned them off for the sum £417-14-5¾.

By now, it would appear that some sort of arrangement about crewing the lifeboat had been made. Lieutenant S. T. Carter, R.N. was in charge of her, whilst Lieutenant S. F. Harmer, who had been on several of the rescues in recent years, was now with the new Yarmouth lifeboat, crewed by Thomas Layton and his company of beachmen.

Lieutenant Carter, who had so far been responsible for saving over fifty lives, had the **Frances Ann** out again on July 21st, 1831. A schooner had been seen to go aground on the Ridge in a strong sou-sou-west wind. The lifeboat launched immediately. So did a yawl from Pakefield, which got to the casualty first. The schooner was the **Sarah** of Brixham, Browning master, which was laden with coal. The crew of six were taken off by the yawl, which then started to fill with water and, but for timely arrival of the lifeboat, would have been swamped. The lifeboat crew were awarded five pounds by the Suffolk Humane Society, whilst the Suffolk Shipwreck Society voted seven pounds to the crew of the Pakefield yawl.

A heavy gale of wind from the south-west on March 6th, 1832, resulted in the loss of the barge **Richard** of London. Bound for Yarmouth with a cargo of timber, when crossing the Barnard Sand a heavy sea shifted her deck cargo to leeward and also filled her. The master decided to make for the recently opened harbour at Lowestoft, but while still a good half mile away another heavy sea carried away her tiller, she broached-to and upset. The wreck drifted north and grounded near Lowestoft Ness with the master and crew of two hanging on. The lifeboat had been launched and Manby's apparatus was ready, but the crew were taken off by the beachmen. Unfortunately one man, Joseph Little, died before help could reach him.

Lowestoft's harbour had only been opened a year, to the great annoyance of some people. Whether through lack of knowledge, or with intent to injure, the report on this wreck issued from Yarmough said the vessel "running for the new harbour at Lowestoft struck upon the bar and upset." The Lowestoft Harbourmaster, Mr. R. B. Mathews took exception to this report and promptly forwarded to the various local papers and the shipping papers in London, a copy of a certificate signed by William Taylor, the master of the barge, which stated that he was "not within a quarter of a mile of the bar when she upset." Four days after the wreck, Thomas Balls, auctioneer, sold materials from it in sixty lots for £27-18-3d. and the hull to G. Gale for £39. Less than a fortnight later, the same auctioneer, on behalf of G. Gale, sold the hull timbers in two hundred and eighty-six lots for £60-11-4½.

It was nearly three years before the lifeboat got her next mention in the papers. The schooner **Bishop Blaze**, Robert Hunter master, was bound from

Hull to London with general cargo. On Sunday, January 18th, 1835, in a south-east gale she went on the Newcome. Four members of the crew got into their long boat and made for the shore, leaving the master and the mate (his son) on board. As soon as the ship was seen to be in trouble a boat had gone off from Pakefield. They picked up four of the men from the schooner's boat, and as it was now dark, took them ashore. Lowestoft lifeboat was immediately notified that two men were still on the wreck. "Lieutenant S. T. Carter, R.N., with the alacrity which that officer had shown in many preceding cases, and accompanied with a brave crew, proceeded to the vessel and after many attempts by rowing and sailing, succeeded in rescuing the two poor fellows from their perilous positions and landed them safely about 10.30 p.m. The vessel was a total loss."

A strong gale from the north-east during the early part of February, 1836, caused the loss of a number of vessels. Early on the fourth two brigs were observed on the Barnards about five miles to the south of the town. Lieutenant Carter soon had a crew assembled and the lifeboat launched and proceeded to the two wrecks. Unfortunately, one boat had completely gone before the lifeboat managed to get there, but from the other, the **Speedwell**, of South Shields, they managed to save the only man left, whom they landed at Kessingland. The lifeboat was then towed about three quarters of a mile along the beach to the north, in order to launch to the assistance of the brig **David Ricardo**, of London, which was lying on the flat. Whilst this was being done, Lieutenant Carter was unfortunately injured severely in the right arm, preventing him from going off again in the boat. However she was soon launched, manned by Lowestoft and Pakefield men and successfully saved the whole crew of seven.

At seven in the evening on the first day of November in 1837, Lieutenant Carter was informed that a brig was on the south-west end of the Newcome and was showing night signals for assistance. A strong south-west gale was blowing accompanied by hail and rain. Two beach yawls tried to launch, but failed to do so. Lieutenant Carter, accompanied by H. B. Disney, Trinity pilot, with the assistance of many of the townspeople, managed to get the lifeboat off and, after three attempts, succeeded in taking out the master, William Bamfield, the crew of nine and four passengers, a Mr. and Miss Richardson, Miss M. A. Beckett and Mr. George Wilson. The brig was the **Bywell** of Newcastle, a new vessel of 250 tons burthen, on her way home from London with a cargo of tea and tobacco valued at over thirty thousand pounds, unfortunately uninsured. The vessel became a total wreck soon after the crew left. About two months later the Leith smack **Sir Walter Scott**, bound for London, lost her rudder. On the tenth of January, 1838, she was see lying at anchor close to the Barnard, flying a signal of distress. The lifeboat launched under Lieutenant Carter in a strong east-north-east gale with snow showers, and proceeded to the vessel. Although the smack was leaking, the Captain and crew refused to leave her, and taking a woman and a boy out of the vessel and signaling the yawl **Seaflower** to stand by the stricken vessel, Lieutenant Carter landed them at Benacre, where the lifeboat remained at the request of the captain in case she was wanted later.

It was not until 1842, that the lifeboat is again mentioned in the press. On the twenty-sixth of that month, at about one o'clock in the afternoon, a vessel named the **Thomas Oliver** was observed on the Inner Newcome. A wind of hurricane force had whipped up huge seas and the lifeboat was only launched with great difficulty. Lieutant Carter, assisted by H. B. Disney and nineteen beachmen, had to use all their skill and strength before they could get to the stranded vessel. Seas were breaking right over the lifeboat, and once Disney was washed overboard, but, holding on to the safety line, he was soon drawn on board again. Letting go his anchor, Carter veered the lifeboat down on the vessel and managed to get a line across to the crew in the rigging. By this means seven of the eight men on board were hauled through the surf into the lifeboat, a distance of about twenty yards. Then her anchor came home and only with difficulty was the lifeboat worked out of the dangerous position she was in, having to pass under the bowspirit of the wreck in order to get clear. The cable was then cut, and full of water, the **Frances Ann** made for the shore, leaving the eighth man, who was the Captain, still on the wreck. As the tide was dropping he was not in great danger and soon afterwards, he was rescued by the Pakefield lifeboat.

The lifeboat, although considerably damaged, made the shore safely, but Lieutenant Carter was so exhausted that he had to be lifted out of the boat and carried to a nearby house where, says Mr. Everitt in his report of the rescue, "the usual means having been resorted to, he was after a few hours so restored as to be able to return to his residence in a chaise". Reports of this rescue, published some fifty years later, claim that this was the last rescue made by the **Frances Ann** The old lady was considered fit enough to race against much newer lifeboats in 1845, giving a very good account of herself, so this claim is doubtful. More likely it was Lieutenant Carter's last rescue.

Whether the **Frances Ann** did carry out other rescues may never be known for certain. Her replacement was not built until 1850, and a lifeboat carried out a rescue from Lowestoft on 17th May, 1843, so it was most possibly her. The casualty on this occasion was the **Farnacres** of Sunderland, Rouse master. On her way from Sunderland to London with coal she was wrecked on the Corton Sands. Newspaper reports at the time merely state "The crew were saved by the lifeboat."

In 1886 a local paper, publishing an autobiography of the Lowestoft cox'n, Robert Hook, claimed that the **Frances Ann** took the crew of twelve or thirteen and a Quaker and a Quakeress out of the Newcastle trader **Bigwell** on the Holm sand in 1848, the vessel knocking off and sinking soon afterwards. No trace of the **Bigwell** has yet been found in the Norfolk or Suffolk papers of the time. The details are very similar to those recorded in the loss of the Newcastle trader **Bywell** on November 1st, 1837. Ten crew and four passengers were saved, and the brig went on her beam ends soon afterwards (see page 17). It is possible that after fifty years Robert Hook got some of his dates a little mixed up.

FRANCES ANN

Summary of Services (so far traced)

24- 2-1808	Unknown collier	no service
14-12-1809	**Catherine** of Sunderland	saved 1
13- 1-1815	**Jeanie** of Hull, sloop.	saved 3
22-10-1820	**Sarah and Caroline** of Woodbridge, sloop	saved 5
	George of London, brig	saved 7
7-12-1821	**Westmoreland** of Stockton, brig	no service
18- 1-1825	**Ann** of ?	saved crew
	Dorset of Ramsgate, sloop	saved part crew
20-10-1825	**Rochester** of North Shields, brig	too late
17- 5-1828	**Fawn** of Sunderland, brig	crew saved from own boat
23-11-1829	**Thomas and Mary** of Newcastle, brig	saved 10
24-11-1829	**Ann** of London, brig	saved 10
26-11-1830	**Clifton** of ? brig	saved 10
21- 7-1831	**Sarah** of Brixham, schooner	assisted to save 6
6- 3-1832	**Richard** of London, barge	no service
18- 1-1835	**Bishop Blaze** of Hull, schooner	saved 2
4- 2-1836	**Speedwell** of South Shields, brig.	saved 1
	David Ricardo of London, brig.	saved 7
1-11-1837	**Bywell** of Newcastle, brig.	saved 14
10- 1-1838	**Sir Walter Scott** of Leith, smack	took 2 ashore
26- 1-1842	**Thomas Oliver** of Sunderland, brig.	saved 7
17- 5-1843	**Farnacres** of Sunderland, snow	saved crew
1848	**Bigwell** of Newcastle (may be **Bywell** above)	saved 12 or 13

VICTORIA 1850-69

"IT was the anniversary of the Suffolk Humane Society and Lifeboat Association on Tuesday last. On this occasion the new lifeboat **Victoria** built by S. Sparham of this town, at 11.00 a.m. commenced an acquaintance with that element in which her future services are to be exerted".

These lines in the "Norfolk Chronicle" of August 31st, 1850, announced the launch of the vessel to replace the lifeboat **Frances Ann**. The report continues - "She is a fine vessel of 42 feet in length, 11 ft. 6 ins. broad and a depth of 3 ft. 11 ins. She took her first trip accompanied by the Society boat from Pakefield, the wind blowing half a gale from the south-west. On her return the crew endeavoured to capsize her by weighting sides and masts, but as an old beachman exclaimed, "She would not budge!". In size the new boat is two feet longer than the **Frances Ann**, her beam and depth being proportionally more, and like her predecessor, she rowed fourteen oars and had the same sail plan. Her cork belt was level with the gunwale, lifelines were fastened along the bulwarks to assist persons entering the boat from the water, and there was a continuous deck fore and aft to enable the crew to get easily from one end of the boat to the other. Her water ballast was confined to a well amidships and she was fitted with relieving valves. She was also fitted with air chambers .

At the anniversary meeting of the society held on the 28th August, 1851, both boats were out again, this time taking about twenty-five ladies and gentlemen in addition to the normal crew. They raced out about a mile beyond the sands and then returned and landed their passengers, the Lowestoft boat opposite Battery Green and the Pakefield boat at the pier. The Lowestoft boat was beaten by the older Pakefield boat "owing to the Lowestoft boat not being supplied with sails suitable to her dimensions". The **Victoria** had inherited a suit of sails from the **Frances Ann.**

On Friday, November 12th, 1852, the Sunderland brig **Wear Packet,** with coals from her home port for London, hit an obstruction when passing through the Stanford Channel. She made water so rapidly that she had to be run on to the Newcome Sands. Two yawls immediately put out but were unable to get near the vessel. Lieutenant Joachim offered to go out with any crew that would man the lifeboat and the Harbour Tug was ready to take them in tow, but the best men were out in the yawls and the rest looked on the case as hopeless. "Was there a chance of saving them we would go" was their reply. By evening the wreck had almost disppeared. The failure of the lifeboat to launch on this occasion caused quite a bit of controversy in the town. It also resulted in the announcement that "Mr. Peto, with the philanthrophy and that goodness of heart which so eminently distinguished him, is about to have a new lifeboat built for the port, which will always be in the harbour in readiness for service". No record of this boat being built has yet been found.

The first known launch of the **Victoria** was on the sixth of January 1853 to the Ipswich brig **Marys,** bound from Sunderland to Ipswich with coals, which drove on to the Holm Sand in a south-west gale. The tug **Imperial**, out under Captain Andrews, the harbour master, picked up the lifeboat outside the harbour and towed her "through tremendous seas and in the teeth of the gale" down to the wreck, which in the meantime had been driven right over the Holm and onto the Newcome Sands. Her crew of six men and a boy were saved, some by the Lowestoft boat, others by the Pakefield boat which arrived on the scene at the same time. The wreck later went to pieces. Mr. Peto donated twenty pounds to the Lowestoft beachmen and D. H. Fry, Esq., ten pounds. A letter in the local paper on these liberal rewards hoped they would stimulate others to follow the example as "the Society managing the lifeboats is at present so poor that it can give only five pounds to those brave fellows on each occasion of going off".

A few months after this launch another brig, the **Mary Young** of Shields, was in trouble. On April 25th, passing down through the Stanford Channel bound for Genoa, the violence of the weather forced her to anchor. At low water she touched the Newcome Sand and unshipped her rudder. Signals of distress brought out the lifeboat, launching for the first time under a new cox'n, Robert Hook. During the next thirty years this giant, who stood six feet three inches, was to earn for himself a reputation as a cox'n second to none. In this instance he saved the crew of ten.

In August, 1854, at the annual Yarmouth Regatta, there was a competition for local lifeboats. Those entered came from Southwold, Pakefield, Lowestoft, Caister, Bacton, Palling, Scratby and Mundesley. Yarmouth beachmen did not enter, the press saying "through fear of being beaten". The first exercise was - "out plugs, fill the boats with water, try to capsize them, then free them from water". The Scratby boat came first, Lowestoft second. Then the boats with sails started in a contest of speed, part of the distance being sailed free from water and part with the boats full, when oars could be used. Here the Caister boat was first, Lowestoft second and Scratby third.

The two local lifeboats became connected with the Royal National Lifeboat Institute in London during the following year. It was considered that a clause in the Merchant Navy Act, due to come into force on May 1st, could alter the management of all Lifeboat Associations. This was clause 459, by which the salvage of life was to take precedence over that of goods, and, if there was no available property from which the salvers could be paid, the Board of Trade were empowered to pay them from the Mercantile Marine Fund, the power of award to be with two Justices of the Peace in the district where the case occured, unless the sum was over £200.

At a meeting of the Lifeboat Society held at the Crown Hotel at Lowestoft on the 5th March, "the desirableness of uniting our local society with the Institute (R.N.L.I.) was taken into consideration and it being considered that the union would operate favourably and be preferable to their remaining a distinct Society receiving aid from the Board of Trade, a resolution was passed accordingly". The London Institute had already sent down several rewards to the crews of the lifeboats and some beach yawls.

At about the same time it was announced that negotiations were in hand with the directors of the Eastern Counties Railway Company and the Norfolk & Lowestoft Railway and Harbour Company, for permission to keep the lifeboat afloat in the harbour and at the annual meeting in September it was resolved "that the Lowestoft boat be kept afloat in the Harbour during the winter, suitably protected by a canvas cover."

In November, 1855, the **Victoria** was concerned in an unusual incident. The brig **Lousia,** of and from Newhaven with timber from Sunderland, got on the Holm Sand. The Harbour Company's tug **Pursuit** towed the lifeboat out, each man being provided with a lifebelt (the first time these are mentioned). Whilst the lifeboat was lying near the casualty, the tide fell and she was left dry upon the sand for something like five hours. The report published at the time says that "men were observed walking to and from the ship - a very unusual sight". (In the reminiscences of Robert Hook, the cox'n, published in a local paper in 1892, he says the lifeboat was aground from 7.00 a.m. until 3.00 p.m. and was swamped by waves.) The **Victoria** refloated on the rising tide and brought the crew of nine ashore. Pakefield lifeboat also launched and stood by, but fortunately was not needed.

The Newcome Sand in a north-east gale was the scene of the next incident in which the **Victoria** was involved. the brig **Tennant** of Stockton, bound for London from Danzig with timber, got on the north part of the sand on January 5th, 1857. For this service the lifeboat was under the command of Captain Richard Joachim, R.N., and rescued the crew of seven. The brig herself was assisted off on the tenth by the beachmen and brought into the Inner Harbour. Early in March she was bought by Robert Westaway, the shipbuilder, for £205. He had her refitted as a snow and sold her to Small & Co., who had her re-registered at Lowestoft. Captain Joachim, who was in charge of the lifeboat for this incident, was Commander of the Lowestoft Coastguards and also a member of the Lifeboat Association Committee of Management. In 1855 Lieutenant J. B. Hockley, who was in charge of the Corton Coastguards was also elected to the Committee of Management and when Joachim was away Hockley took charge of the lifeboat. Captain Joachim still "had management of the boat" in 1859 and at the Annual Meeting of the Suffolk Humane Society and the Lowestoft and Pakefield Lifeboat Association held in November of that year, while Cox'n Hook reported on the work of rescue, Joachim reported on the inefficient state of the Lowestoft boat's sails and asked for new ones. The inefficency of the sails must have been obvious to everyone after the trouble they gave during two services on the 26th October, just a few days before the meeting.

Early on that morning the Dundee schooner **Lord Douglas** (James White, Captain) from Bowness for Doit with pig iron, was driven by a south-west gale onto Corton Beach. Coastguards were unable to reach her with the rocket apparatus, so the lifeboat was called out. When they arrived at the wreck they found the vessel sunk and the crew of five in the rigging. They succeeded in getting them all off, but as the foresail had split, they beached the lifeboat at Corton and walked back to town. (Some reports say they beached near the Warren House).

Later the same day, the Glasgow schooner **Silva** which had been riding at anchor under the Holm Sand, parted from her anchor and drove onto the Corton Bank. The Lowestoft crew again assembled, complete with a new foresail and trudged off along the beach to where they had left the life-boat. (Hook in 1892 says they sailed up in a yawl). Meanwhile, the Pakefield boat had been launched and ran down to the scene, aided by the gale. The reporter on the spot said "It was an exciting scene to see her (the Lowestoft boat) beating up and a cheering sight to see the gallant Pakefield men with their boat running down to the same spot. By some means the Pakefield boat overshot the mark, but the Lowestoft boat was more successful and, having come to windward, wore down and through tremendous breakers which at times covered her, and rescued the crew of four. Yet another schooner was seen in distress, this time outside the sands, but as the Lowestoft boat set off for this vessel, her foresail was again split by the strength of the gale, so she made for Yarmouth with the **Silva's** crew and handed them over to the care of the Shipwrecked Fishermens Society, where they were duly "supplied with restoratives, dry clothes, food, etc." and later sent home. The Pakefield boat went out to the third schooner (name unknown) and towed her through the Gatway to safety.

Within the week the **Victoria** was out again in another heavy gale, blowing from the south-south-west, to the steamer **Shamrock** of Dublin, which went on the south-east part of the Holm Sand. This rescue is graphically described and illustrated in the "Illustrated London News" of November 26th, 1859.

"The Lowestoft beachmen seeing the sea breaking heavily over her, and from their experience knowing that no time was to be lost, collected their people and immediately launched the lifeboat which is in connection with the Royal National Lifeboat Institute, for their rescue. When the lifeboat reached the steamer, the sea was breaking over the masthead, but she was providentially enabled to anchor in a most advantageous position ahead of her and although the sea broke over her and repeatedly filled her, this excellent lifeboat as often, in her buoyancy clearing herself of the seas was at length, with difficulty, enabled to approach the steamer. A communication was then by ropes established with the wreck and the whole crew of fourteen were hauled by the lines through the sea to the lifeboat and brought safely to the shore".

For this rescue, the Institue awarded their silver medals to Richard (sic) Hook, Francis Smith, Richard Butcher, Alfred Mewse, Thomas Liffen, James Butcher and William Rose.

Two years later, in November, 1861, the **Victoria** had her busiest month. On the second she went out to the Whitby schooner **Fly** in distress off Ness Point in a strong gale. Some of the lifeboatmen boarded the schooner and helped the crew of the vessel to get her safely into harbour. Eight days later the Lowestoft and Pakefield boats between them saved the crew of eleven of the barque **Undaunted** of Aberdeen, but although they tried to save the vessel, she sank on the way into the harbour. On the fourteenth two vessels, the pilot cutter **Whim** of Yarmouth and the lugger **Saucy Lass** were in distress on the weather side of the Holm Sand. The **Victoria** was launched, saved the crew of seven from the **Whim** and was then towed down to the lugger by the tug **Powerful** (Captain Porter) and saved the crew of eleven.

The tug **Powerful,** this time under the Harbour Master, Captain Rivers, assisted the lifeboat again early in 1862, when she towed the **Victoria** out to the Corton sand. The brigantine **Matilda,** of Stockholm, had gone ashore during a gale and some of the crew and the pilot managed to get ashore early in the morning in one of the ship's boats and gave the alarm (no reason is given for not putting up distress flares). The lifeboat was able to save the Captain and three others. For this rescue the Institute awarded its thanks on Vellum to Captain Rivers.

"Early in the morning of January 13th" wrote Dr. Worthington in the 'Times' of January 17th, 1866, "a vessel drove on the far end of the Holm Sand and lay exposed to violence of a severe gale from the south-west with heavy seas. Twelve men were seen on board. The lifeboat put out and battled her way out, but was unable to get near, owing to the heavy masts and spars floating by the side of the wreck. The lifeboat was compelled to cut her cable and leave the wreck. On her return to harbour she took on a new anchor cable. She was then towed out again by the **Rainbow** (which Dr. Worthington had now boarded). The atmosphere was thick from fog and rain and the gale still continued. When the lifeboat got back to the wreck they found nothing but the bare stern of the vessel, the remainder being buried in the sands and the breakers, apparently without a human creature upon it. The tug continued to tow as fast as possible and men were seen in the shelter. The lifeboat approached the wreck just as some of the crew were washed off in the direction of the lifeboat. Altogether eight men were rescued out of twelve".

This was the worthy Doctor's description of the wreck of the Austrian brig **Osip** of Fiume. She was bound from Falmouth, with a cargo of maize, for Hull. The Falmouth pilot was still on board, and he was among those rescued but, unfortunately, he died soon afterwards. The Institute's report of the incident says that the yawl **Young Prince** put out first, but her services were refused, as were those of the lifeboat. In fact the captain of the brig was said to have threatened his crew with a revolver, but he was overpowered. By then the brig was awash and the lifeboat drove right over her and saved all twelve. The same day, the Gorleston lifeboat, putting out to the assistance of a wrecked vessel, was capsized in the surf with the loss of twelve of her crew of nineteen.

Details of the **Osip** rescue were forwarded to the Austrian government, but as that country was at war with both Prussia and Italy at the time, the matter was put on one side, then forgotten in the trials and tribulations of defeat.

Some years later the matter was revived and on September 7th, 1892, twenty-six years after the rescue, the Mayor of Lowestoft, Mr. B. M. Bradbeer, distributed awards to the cox'n and surviving members of the crew. Bob Hook was presented with three guineas and a pair of binoculars, suitably inscribed. The crew were given one guinea each, for each time that they had gone out. If the crew member had died in the meantime, the award was given to a relative. Controversy over these payments raged in the local press for several weeks. Some men said that they had been out twice but had only been paid for one trip, others said that men had received payment who had not been out at all and some who went out were missed off the list.

On August 22nd of the following year, silver medals were publicly presented to the Lowestoft lifeboat "Sea Lions", in the South Pier Pavilion. As the Austro-Hungarian government did not have a suitable medal and would need a special Act of Parliament to authorise one, the silver medal was made privately. The presentation list on this occasion differed from the earlier one and as there were no complaints in the press aftewards, it must have been fairly accurate. The men out on both trips were shown as:- Bob Hook, David Cook, Samuel Mewse, Robert James Yallop, George Yallop, Richard Butcher, Alfred Mewse, W. Smith and James Ayers. Those who went on the first trip only were:- Joseph Swan, John Mewse, William Gallant, James Clarke, Samuel Mewse, William Norman, William Norman Jun., William Burwood Capps, William Capps, Charles Liffen, Thomas S. Rose, John Gurney, and William Swan Rose. The following went on the second trip only:- Edward Ellis, William Spurgeon, Charles Allerton, Samuel Mewse, James Yallop, George Clarke, Samuel Taylor, Benjamin Butcher and William Ayers.

Incidentally, although nothing was said at the time, the inscription on Hook's binoculars was not correct. It read:- "To Robert William Hook, coxswain of the Lowestoft lifeboat **Laetitia**, from the Imperial and Royal Austrian Government in recognition of the valuable service rendered to the crew of the Austrian brig OSIP on the 13th January 1866". The lifeboat was the **Victoria,** which was not renamed **Laetitia** until early in 1869.

Another Mediterranean brig was in trouble in May, 1867. This was the **Amicizia** of Genoa, which went on the bar of the Stanford Channel on the 23rd May, in a strong breeze. Both the Lowestoft and Pakefield boats were launched, the **Victoria** saving ten and the Pakefield boat the remainder, numbering four. Six months later, on November 17th, the Yarmouth brigantine **Medora** parted from her anchors and drove on the north end of the Newcome Sand. Three of the crew took to one of the ship's boats and were lost, the remaining two men waited for the lifeboat and were saved, just before the wreck broke up.

In 1868 a lady, un-named, presented the Institute with the cost of a lifeboat, so early in 1869 "the large sailing lifeboat on this station was appropriated to that gift, and the boat was renamed **Laetitia**". The remainder of her story follows under that name.

LAETITIA (ex-VICTORIA) 1869-76

THE first launch of the boat under her new name was on January 29th, 1869 when, early in the morning, the Shields brig **Queen of the Tyne** went on Corton Sands. Laden with coal, she was on her way to London when she struck in a south-west gale. By the time the **Laetitia** got out to her, she was on her beam ends, and the seas were breaking right over her. The crew of eight were in the rigging, anxiously watching the approaching lifeboat and wondering how she was going to get to them. Due to the rise and fall of the brig on the heavy swell, the yards dipping in the water made it very dangerous for any boat to get near. In spite of the danger, however, the crew were eventually taken off by way of the main topgallant yard, which at times threatened to go right through the lifeboat.

A few days later, on February 1st, another vessel was wrecked on the Corton Sands. This was the **Horace E. Bell,** a schooner owned at Appledore and bound from Fecamp for Yarmouth with a cargo of barley. The crew were able to launch their own boat and made Yarmouth safely. Unaware that the vessel had been abandoned, Hook put out in the **Laetitia** but when they reached the wreck all they found were the ship's pets, a cat and a dog, so these were duly "rescued" and brought ashore.

Some days later, the Whitby brig **Beatrix** anchored in Corton Roads to wait for a north-easter to blow itself out. Instead of easing, however, the gale increased and by the thirteenth conditions had become so bad that the crew were forced to cut away the mainmast. Not long afterwards, distress signals were hoisted. Hook took the **Laetitia** out under tow of one of the harbour tugs, possibly the first **Imperial,** and the brig was assisted into harbour.

Early in the following month, the Teignmouth registered schooner **Amelia** was making her way, in ballast, from Torquay, where she was owned, to Hartlepool. During a strong nor-nor-east gale she struck hard on the Holm Sand, on March 3rd, and soon went to pieces, the crew of eight being picked up by the Rye schooner **Anna Lousia.** The **Laetitia** had been launched as soon as the **Amelia** was seen to be in trouble and coming up with the **Anna Lousia,** took off the **Amelia's** surviviors and landed them at Lowestoft.

After five launches (Including one as the **Victoria**) during the first three months of 1869, there was quite a long gap before the lifeboat was called out again. On December 14th, the schooner **Adina,** which was registered in London but owned at Falmouth, was passing well loaded with a mixed cargo of coal and arsenic, when she drove down onto the sands near the East Holm buoy. The **Laetitia** was towed out into a strong sou'west gale and saved the crew of eight. The Pakefield lifeboat **Sisters** was also launched to the aid of the **Adina.**

A north-east gale was responbile for another schooner going onto the Holm Sands ten days later. This was the **Agathe Scheibert** of Stettin. The **Laetitia** was towed out by the paddle tug **Rainbow** and succeeded in saving the master and crew of ten. For many years two nameboards from this vessel decorated the front of the Old Company of Beachmen's 'shod'.

On September 21st, 1870, the cod-smack **Thomas and William,** owned by Messrs, W. & S. Groom of Harwich, was wrecked on the Faroes. The crew of twelve were saved. The smack **Olive,** Thomas Calver, master, also owned by Groom of Harwich took three of the shipwrecked men on board for the homeward journey, the remaining nine being distributed among other

Harwich boats that were on the Faroe grounds. With a cargo of eighty score of cod fish, a ton of salt cod and some live halibut in her well, the **Olive** headed for home. On the afternoon of October 12th, the **Olive** entered Corton Gatway, the weather clear and the sou-west wind just strong enough to cause the master to single reef the foresail. Suddenly, at about 4.30 p.m. the smack struck what the master thought was wreck. An anchor was dropped, but before it could hold, she was driven on the sand near the Corton Spit buoy. An ensign was put in the rigging and the Corton light-ship fired rockets. Both Lowestoft and Corton boats were launched and raced out to the casualty, the **Laetitia** getting there first and, being the bigger boat, took off twelve men. Three other men were taken off by the Corton boat (presumably the three survivors of the **Thomas and William**.) When the two lifeboats were close inshore, these three were transferred from the Corton to the Lowestoft boat and landed at Lowestoft about 8.30 p.m. being taken to the Sailor's Home.

Wreck registers held at the Greenwich Maritime Museum show the whole crew of the **Olive** as being rescued by the **Laetitia,** whilst the Corton boat **Husband** is credited with rescuing the members of the crew of the **Thomas and William,** which is shown as being wrecked on the Corton Sands at the same time as the **Olive**. This is, of course, wrong. Thanks to the librarian of the "Suffolk Mercury" I have been able to get the true story of the loss of these two vessels.

Less than a week later the **Laetitia** was again out near the Corton Spit buoy and another dog was included in the rescue list. On October 18th the brig **Glenora** of Scarborough, bound from Shields to Rochester with coal, went onto the Corton Sands near the **Olive** in a sou-west gale. The eight members of the crew, together with ship's dog, were rescued.

A third vessel went ashore in the Gat on December 14th. This was another Scarborough vessel, the barque **Forest Flower**, a vessel of 518 tons, which was on her way from Almeria to Newcastle with esparto grass. The crew of fifteen were saved by the Lowestoft No. 1 lifeboat, which was the **Laetitia.**

Corton Sands was the site of the first casualty of 1871. The **Lizzie Ann** of Sunderland, outward from that port with coal for Alexandria, struck the sands late on January 23rd. The crew left the ship in their own boat, with the loss of one man. They made Lowestoft safely, passing the lifeboat in the darkness.

Records show a gap of nearly two years before the lifeboat was called out again. This trip turned out to be one of the most difficult and dangerous that Cox'n Hook had had for some years. On November 13th, 1872, the Drobak brig **Expedite** was driven on to the Holm Sands in a north-east gale. The **Laetitia** was towed out, probably by the **Rainbow**, into terrific seas. At first she was unable to relieve herself fast enough of the seas that poured into her. Conditions were so bad in fact that one of the crew, Henry Hall, had his leg broken. Out at the wreck, the lifeboat crew found the casualty surrounded by fallen masts and spars. Approaching from windward, the lifeboat anchored and gradually veered down to the vessel. Working his way carefully through the wreckage, Hook managed to take off the whole crew of ten. For this rescue, Cox'n Robert Hook was awarded his second Service Clasp.

By now Lowestoft had two lifeboats. As intimated above, under the rescue of the **Forest Flower,** the **Laetitia** was the No. 1 boat, but she was considered too big to be worked by oars for inshore work,, so a 32 foot boat was stationed here in 1870. This was the **George**, and she shared the honours with the **Laetitia** on the next service call.

On March 18th, 1873, during a strong gale from the North-east, the schooner **Celine** of Gravelines went on the Holm Sands. Hook went out in a yawl, but the crew refused to leave. As the weather got worse Hook took the **Laetitia** out and this time the crew came off, but the master still said that he was not leaving his ship (some accounts say that he was drunk). The weather continued to worsen so Hook went out again later, but because of lack of water, he took the number 2 boat, the **George** and he managed to force the captain to leave.

The anniversary meeting of the Suffolk Humane Society and the Lowestoft and Pakefield Lifeboat Association took place on August 20th. As usual the morning of that day was spent inspecting the lifeboats and then watching them being exercised. During the meeting that followed it was moved "that for the future the Society bear the name of the 'Lowestoft and Pakefield Branch of the National Lifeboat Institute', and that gear, houses and other property belonging to the Society be transferred to the National Lifeboat Institute".

At the meeting, Robert Hook, the Lowestoft Coxswain, was presented with his second Service Clasp and also a vellum expressing admiration for his bravery in rescuing the crew of the **Expedite** during the previous winter.

There was one more launch in 1873 when, on November 11th, the schooner **Levant,** bound from Goole for Dartmouth with coal, went on to the Newcome. Pakefield Beach Company, assisted by the paddle tug **Rainbow** successfully got the vessel off and into harbour, whilst the Lowestoft and Kessingland lifeboats stood by.

During the next two years the boat made only two service launches, but in neither of these cases did she carry out any actual service. On December 20th 1874, she launched to the brig **Sarah** of Whitby, which was bound from Hartlepool to London with coal. The **Sarah** went on to the Corton Sands, but the crew were saved without the lifeboat being required. The second of these launches was to the ship **China**, which went on the Cross Sand on the night of March 6th, 1875. Several lightships sent up distress signals, resulting in lifeboats being launched at California, Caister, Gorleston and Lowestoft

Four tugs also put out, from Gorleston. The Caister lifeboat was the first on the scene so she was engaged, with the tugs, to get the vessel off. This they managed to do on the following night.

The final service by the **Laetitia,** now twenty-six years old, was carried out on January 14th, 1876. While passing outside the Corton, on her way from Shields to her home port, the three masted schooner **George Smeed** of Rochester lost her foremast. The **Laetitia** put out under Bob Hook and, according to the Lifeboat Institute records, they got the schooner safely into Lowestoft. The service board for the **Laetitia,** which can be seen in the Lifeboat Social Club building at the end of Hamilton Road, says that the lifeboat accompanied the schooner to Rochester.

Institute records show that from 1855 when they took over the Lowestoft station until she was renamed in 1869, the **Victoria** saved one hundred and thirty-seven lives. She had saved at least thirteen before the institute took over and as the **Laetitia** she saved a further ninety-two, which gives a total of at least two hundred and forty-two lives saved during twenty-six years of service.

Below are listed all the known launches by the boat, under both names. Robert Hook first sailed as cox'n on the launch to the **Mary Young,** on April 25th, 1853. He was still cox'n in December, 1876, when the new No. 1 lifeboat, **Samuel Plimsoll,** took over from the **Laetitia.**

LAUNCHES AS VICTORIA

Date	Vessel	Result
6- 1-1853	**Marys,** brig of Ipswich.	
	Assisted by Pakefield boat	Saved 6
25- 4-1853	**Mary Young,** brig of Shields.	Saved 10
7-11-1855	**Lousia,** brig of Newhaven	Saved 9
5- 1-1857	**Tennant,** brig of Stockton	Saved 8
6- 1-1857	**Darlington,** brig of Shields	No service
27- 9 1857	**Elizabeth,** schooner of Portmadoc	No service
25- 2-1858	**Oswy,** brig of Shoreham	Saved 12
8- 3-1858	**Orwell,** schooner of Arbroath	Landed crew
	Friendship, brig	Assisted
26-10-1859	**Lord Douglas,** schooner of Dundee	Saved 5
	Silva, schooner of Glasgow	Saved 4
1-11-1859	**Shamrock,** steamer of Dublin	Saved 14
28- 5-1860	**Three Brothers,** sloop of Goole	Saved 5
5-1860	**Rapid,** brig of Portsmouth	Saved 8
25- 7-1861	**St. Michel,** brig of Marans	Saved 8
2-11-1861	**Fly,** schooner of Whitby	Saved 4

10-11-1861	**Undaunted,** barque of Aberdeen. With Pakefield boat	Saved 11
14-11-1861	**Whim,** pilot cutter of Yarmouth	Saved 7
	Saucy Lass, lugger of Lowestoft	Saved 11
26- 3-1862	**Matilda,** brigantine of Stockholm	Saved 4
21- 2-1865	**Gilbert Alphonse,** lugger	?
20- 3-1865	**Pfeil,** schooner of Blankenesse	Saved 7
15- 8-1865	**Light of the Harem,** brigantine of Whitstable	Saved 4
13- 1-1866	**Osip,** brig of Fiume	Saved 8
31- 1-1866	**Royal Union,** brig of Sunderland	No service
12-12-1866	**William and Mary,** lugger of Yarmouth	Saved 2
23- 5-1867	**Amicizia,** brig of Genoa.	Saved 10
17-11-1867	**Medora,** brigantine of Yarmouth	Saved 2
17- 1-1869	**Nautilus,** smack of Lowestoft	Saved 4

LAUNCHES AS LAETITIA

29- 1-1869	**Queen of the Tyne,** brig of Shields.	Saved 8
1- 2-1869	**Horace E. Bell** schooner of Bideford	Saved dog and cat
13- 2-1869	**Beatrix,** brig of Whitby	Saved 7
3- 3-1869	**Amelia,** schooner of Teignmouth	Landed 8
14-12-1869	**Adina,** schooner of London	Saved 8
24-12-1869	**Agathe Scheibert,** schooner of Stettin	Saved 11
12-10-1870	**Olive,** smack of Harwich	Saved 12
18-10-1870	**Glenora,** brig of Scarborough	Saved 8
14-12-1870	**Forest Flower,** barque of Scarborough	Saved 15
23- 1-1871	**Lizzie Ann,** of Sunderland	No service
13-11-1872	**Expedite,** brig of Drobak	Saved 10
18- 3-1873	**Celine,** schooner of Gravelines	Saved 5
11-11-1873	**Levant,** schooner of Goole	No service
20-12-1874	**Sarah,** brig of Whitby	No service
6- 3-1875	**China,** ship of ?	No service
14- 1-1876	**George Smeed,** schooner of Rochester	Escorted

A local paper dated April 16th, 1892, notes that a brig the **Answer,** was in trouble off Corton some time in 1870. They say the yawl **Mosquito** went out and then called the lifeboat, which saved the crew. No trace of this rescue has so far come to hand.

The same paper also records Hook taking the lifeboat out to the **Rock Scorpion** and rescuing the crew. Again no trace of this in the lifeboat records, but it may have been one of the yawl rescues.

INDEX OF SHIPS NAMES

ADINA (London)	26, 30
AGATHE SCHEIBERT (Stettin)	26, 30
AGNES CROSS (lifeboat)	10
AMELIA (Teignmouth)	26, 30
AMICIZIA (Genoa)	25, 30
ANN (-)	14, 19
ANN (London)	15, 19
ANNA LOUISA (Rye)	26
ANSWER (-)	30
BEATRIX (Whitby)	26, 30
BIGWELL (Newcastle) see BYWELL	
BISHOP BLAZE (Hull)	16, 19
BYWELL (Newcastle)	17, 19
CATHERINE (Sunderland)	10, 19
CELINE (Gravelines)	28, 30
CHINA (-)	28, 30
CLIFTON (-)	15, 19
DARLINGTON (Shields)	29
DAVID RICARDO (London)	17, 19
DORSET (Ramsgate)	14, 19
ECHO (Shields)	10
ELIZABETH (Portmadoc)	29
EXPEDITE (Drobak)	27, 28, 30
FARNARCES (Sunderland)	18, 19
FAWN (Sunderland)	15, 19
FLY (Whitby)	23, 29
FOREST FLOWER (Scarborough)	27, 30
FRANCES ANN (lifeboat)	8-19, 20
FRIENDSHIP (-)	29
GEORGE (London)	12, 19
GEORGE (lifeboat)	28
GEORGE SMEED (Rochester)	29, 30
GILBERT ALPHONSE (-)	30
GLENORA (Scarborough)	27, 30
HOGGETT (-)	10
HORACE E. BELL (Bideford)	26, 30
HUSBAND (lifeboat)	27
IMPERIAL (tug)	20, 26
JANE (Hull) see JEANIE	
JEANIE (Hull)	11, 19
JOHN & MARY MEIKLAM OF GLADSWOOD (lifeboat)	10
LAETITIA (lifeboat)	25-30
LEVANT (Goole)	28, 30
LIGHT OF THE HAREM (Whitstable)	30
LIZZIE ANN (Sunderland)	27, 30
LORD DOUGLAS (Dundee)	22, 29
LOUISA (Newhaven)	21, 29
LOWESTOFT LIFEBOAT	2
MARIA (Newcastle)	10,
MARY'S (Ipswich)	20, 29
MARY SCOTT (lifeboat)	10
MARY YOUNG (Shields)	20, 29
MATILDA (Stockholm)	23, 30
MEDORA (Yarmouth)	25, 30
MICHAEL STEPHENS (lifeboat)	10
MOSQUITO (Yawl)	30
NAUTILUS (Lowestoft)	30
OLIVE (Harwich)	26, 30
ORWELL (Arbroath)	29
OSIP (Fiume)	24, 30
OSWY (Shoreham)	29
PFEIL (Blankenesse)	30
POWERFUL (tug)	23
PURSUIT (tug)	21
QUEEN OF THE TYNE (Shields)	25, 30
RAINBOW (tug)	24, 26, 27, 28
RAPID (Portsmouth)	29
RICHARD (London)	16, 19
ROCK SCORPION (-)	30
ROCHESTER (Shields)	14, 19
ROYAL UNION (Sunderland)	30
ST MICHEL (Marams)	29
SAMUEL PLIMSOLL (lifeboat)	29
SARAH (Brixham)	16, 19
SARAH (Whitby)	28, 30
SARAH & CAROLINE (Woodbridge)	12, 19
SAUCY LASS (Lowestoft)	23, 30
SEAFLOWER (Yawl)	17
SEAMAN'S ASSISTANCE (Yawl)	13
SHAMROCK (Dublin)	23, 29
SILVA (Glasgow)	22, 29
SIR WALTER SCOTT (Leith)	17, 19
SISTERS (lifeboat)	26
SPEEDWELL (Shields)	17, 19
SYLPH (Sunderland)	10
TENNANT (Stockton & Lowestoft)	22, 29
THOMAS & MARY (Newcastle)	15, 19
THOMAS & WILLIAM (Harwich)	26
THOMAS OLIVER (Sunderland)	18, 19
THREE BROTHERS (Goole)	29
UNDAUNTED (Aberdeen)	23, 30
VICTORIA (Lifeboat)	19-25
WEAR PACKET (Sunderland)	20
WESTMORELAND (Stockton)	13, 19
WHIM (Yarmouth)	23, 30
WILLIAM & MARY (Yarmouth)	30
YOUNG PRINCE (Yawl)	24

INDEX OF PERSONS & INSTITUTIONS

Barcham, Batchelor (boatbuilders)	7, 9
Bowness, Rev. Francis	2, 5
Carter, Lieut. Samuel Thomas. R.N.	13, 15 - 18
Disney, H. B (pilot)	11, 13, 17, 18
Greathead, Henry (boatbuilder)	2
Harmer, Lieut.	14, 15, 16
Hockley, Lieut. J. B.	22
Hook, Robert (Coxn)	18, 21, 23, 24, 25, 28, 29
Joachin, Capt. Richard	20, 22
Lowestoft Lifeboat Society	2, 7
Lowestoft & Pakefield Branch, National Lifeboat Institute	28
Lukin, Lionel	4, 5, 6, 8
Pakefield Beach Company	28
Reed, Capt. Gilfred Lawson	3, 4, 6
Ritson, Rev. Bartholomew	11
Rous, Lord	7, 8
Royal National Lifeboat Institue	21, 23, 28
Sparham, Samuel (boatbuilder)	19
Sparrow, Robert	2 - 7
Spurdens, Rev. W.	7, 8
Suffolk Association for the Preservation of Lives of Shipwrecked Seamen	14, 16
Suffolk Humane Society	7, 8, 10, 11, 12, 13, 15, 16
Suffolk Humane Society and Pakefield Lifeboat Association	19, 21, 22, 28